World Economic and Financial Surveys

REGIONAL ECONOMIC OUTLOOK

SUB-SAHARAN AFRICA

The Big Funding Squeeze

2023
APRIL

Cataloging-in-Publication Data
IMF Library

Names: International Monetary Fund, publisher.
Title: Regional economic outlook. Sub-Saharan Africa: the big funding squeeze.
Other titles: Sub-Saharan Africa : the big funding squeeze. | World economic and financial surveys.

Description: Washington, DC : International Monetary Fund, 2023. | World economic and financial surveys. | Apr. 2023. | Includes bibliographical references.

Identifiers: ISBN 9798400235641 (English Paper)
9798400235771 (ePub)
9798400236044 (Web PDF)

Subjects: LCSH: Africa, Sub-Saharan—Economic conditions. | Economic forecasting—Africa, Sub-Saharan. | Economic development—Africa, Sub-Saharan. | Africa, Sub-Saharan—Economic policy.
Classification: LCC HC800.R4456 2023

The *Regional Economic Outlook: Sub-Saharan Africa* is published twice a year, in the spring and fall, to review developments in sub-Saharan Africa. Both projections and policy considerations are those of the IMF staff and do not necessarily represent the views of the IMF, its Executive Board, or IMF Management.

Publication orders may be placed online or through the mail:
International Monetary Fund, Publication Services
P.O. Box 92780, Washington, DC 20090, U.S.A.
T. +(1) 202.623.7430
F. +(1) 202.623.7201
publications@IMF.org
IMFbookstore.org
elibrary.IMF.org

Find all published *Regional Economic Outlook: Sub-Saharan Africa*
https://www.imf.org/en/Publications/REO/SSA

Contents

FIGURES

TABLES

STATISTICAL TABLES

Acknowledgments

The April 2023 issue of the *Regional Economic Outlook: Sub-Saharan Africa* was prepared by a team led by Wenjie Chen and under the supervision of Luc Eyraud and Catherine Pattillo.

The team included Hany Abdel-Latif, Anna Belianska, Marijn Bolhuis, Balazs Csonto, Cleary Haines, Saanya Jain, Laurent Kemoe, Hamza Mighri, Saad Quayyum, Moustapha Mbohou Mama, Pritha Mitra, Henry Rawlings, Ivanova Reyes, Andrew Tiffin, and Qianqian Zhang.

Charlotte Vazquez was responsible for document production, with assistance from Yao Nourdine Ouattara.

The editing and production were overseen by Cheryl Toksoz of the Communications Department.

Country Groupings

Sub-Saharan Africa: Member Countries of Groupings

Oil Exporters	Other Resource-Intensive Countries	Non-Resource-Intensive Countries	Middle-Income Countries	Low-Income Countries	Countries in Fragile and Conflict-Affected Situations[1]
Angola	Botswana	Benin	Angola	Burkina Faso	Burkina Faso
Cameroon	Burkina Faso	Burundi	Benin	Burundi	Burundi
Chad	Central African	Cabo Verde	Botswana	Central	Cameroon
Congo, Republic of	Republic	Comoros	Cabo Verde	African Republic	Central African
Equatorial Guinea	Congo,	Côte d'Ivoire	Cameroon	Chad	Republic
Gabon	Democratic	Eswatini	Comoros	Congo,	Chad
Nigeria	Republic of the	Ethiopia	Congo, Republic of	Democratic	Comoros
South Sudan	Eritrea	Gambia, The	Côte d'Ivoire	Republic of the	Congo, Democratic
	Ghana	Guinea-Bissau	Equatorial Guinea	Eritrea	Republic of the
	Guinea	Kenya	Eswatini	Ethiopia	Congo, Republic of
	Liberia	Lesotho	Gabon	Gambia, The	Eritrea
	Mali	Madagascar	Ghana	Guinea	Ethiopia
	Namibia	Malawi	Kenya	Guinea-Bissau	Guinea-Bissau
	Niger	Mauritius	Lesotho	Liberia	Mali
	Sierra Leone	Mozambique	Mauritius	Madagascar	Mozambique
	South Africa	Rwanda	Namibia	Malawi	Niger
	Tanzania	São Tomé	Nigeria	Mali	Nigeria
	Zambia	and Príncipe	São Tomé	Mozambique	South Sudan
	Zimbabwe	Senegal	and Príncipe	Niger	Zimbabwe
		Seychelles	Senegal	Rwanda	
		Togo	Seychelles	Sierra Leone	
		Uganda	South Africa	South Sudan	
			Zambia	Tanzania	
				Togo	
				Uganda	
				Zimbabwe	

[1] Fragile and conflict-affected situations as classified by the World Bank, *Classification of Fragile and Conflict-Affected Situations, FY2023.*

Sub-Saharan Africa: Member Countries of Regional Groupings

The West African Economic and Monetary Union (WAEMU)	Economic and Monetary Community of Central African States (CEMAC)	Common Market for Eastern and Southern Africa (COMESA)	East African Community (* = EAC-5)	Southern African Development Community (SADC)	Southern African Customs Union (SACU)	Economic Community of West African States (ECOWAS)
Benin	Cameroon	Burundi	*Burundi	Angola	Botswana	Benin
Burkina Faso	Central African	Comoros	*Kenya	Botswana	Eswatini	Burkina Faso
Côte d'Ivoire	Republic	Congo,	*Rwanda	Comoros	Lesotho	Cabo Verde
Guinea-Bissau	Chad	Democratic	South Sudan	Congo,	Namibia	Côte d'Ivoire
Mali	Congo, Republic of	Republic of the	*Tanzania	Democratic	South Africa	Gambia, The
Niger	Equatorial Guinea	Eritrea	*Uganda	Republic of the		Ghana
Senegal	Gabon	Eswatini		Eswatini		Guinea
Togo		Ethiopia		Lesotho		Guinea-Bissau
		Kenya		Madagascar		Liberia
		Madagascar		Malawi		Mali
		Malawi		Mauritius		Niger
		Mauritius		Mozambique		Nigeria
		Rwanda		Namibia		Senegal
		Seychelles		Seychelles		Sierra Leone
		Uganda		South Africa		Togo
		Zambia		Tanzania		
		Zimbabwe		Zambia		
				Zimbabwe		

Assumptions and Conventions

The following conventions are used in this publication:

In tables, ellipsis points (. . .) indicate "not available," and 0 or 0.0 indicates "zero" or "negligible." Minor discrepancies between sums of constituent figures and totals are due to rounding.

An en dash (–) between years or months (for example, 2011–12 or January–June) indicates the years or months covered, including the beginning and ending years or months; a slash or virgule (/) between years or months (for example, 2011/12) indicates a fiscal or financial year, as does the abbreviation FY (for example, FY 2012).

"Billion" means a thousand million; "trillion" means a thousand billion.

"Basis points (bps)" refer to hundredths of 1 percentage point (for example, 25 basis points are equivalent to ¼ of 1 percentage point).

As used in this publication, the term "country" does not in all cases refer to a territorial entity that is a state as understood by international law and practice. As used here, the term also covers some territorial entities that are not states but for which statistical data are maintained on a separate and independent basis.

The boundaries, colors, denominations, and any other information shown on the maps do not imply, on the part of the International Monetary Fund, any judgment on the legal status of any territory or any endorsement or acceptance of such boundaries.

Sub-Saharan Africa: Country Abbreviations

AGO	Angola	CPV	Cabo Verde	LSO	Lesotho	SLE	Sierra Leone
BDI	Burundi	ERI	Eritrea	MDG	Madagascar	SSD	South Sudan
BEN	Benin	ETH	Ethiopia	MLI	Mali	STP	São Tomé and Príncipe
BFA	Burkina Faso	GAB	Gabon	MOZ	Mozambique	SWZ	Eswatini
BWA	Botswana	GHA	Ghana	MUS	Mauritius	SYC	Seychelles
CAF	Central African Republic	GIN	Guinea	MWI	Malawi	TCD	Chad
CIV	Côte d'Ivoire	GMB	Gambia, The	NAM	Namibia	TGO	Togo
CMR	Cameroon	GNB	Guinea-Bissau	NER	Niger	TZA	Tanzania
COD	Congo, Democratic Republic of the	GNQ	Equatorial Guinea	NGA	Nigeria	UGA	Uganda
COG	Congo, Republic of	KEN	Kenya	RWA	Rwanda	ZAF	South Africa
COM	Comoros	LBR	Liberia	SEN	Senegal	ZMB	Zambia
						ZWE	Zimbabwe

Executive Summary

A funding squeeze has hit the region hard. Persistent global inflation and tighter monetary policies have led to higher borrowing costs for sub-Saharan African countries and have placed greater pressure on exchange rates. Indeed, no country has been able to issue a Eurobond since spring 2022.

The funding squeeze aggravates a protracted trend that has been years in the making. The interest burden on public debt is rising, because of a greater reliance on expensive market-based funding combined with a long-term decline in aid budgets.

The lack of financing affects a region that is already struggling with elevated macroeconomic imbalances. Public debt and inflation are at levels not seen in decades, with double-digit inflation present in half of countries—eroding household purchasing power, striking at the most vulnerable, and adding to social pressures. Estimates suggest that 132 million people were acutely food-insecure in 2022.

In this context, the economic recovery has been interrupted. Growth in sub-Saharan Africa will decline to 3.6 percent in 2023. Amid a global slowdown, activity is expected to decelerate for a second year in a row. Still, this headline figure masks significant variation across the region. Many countries will register a small pickup in growth this year, especially non-resource-intensive economies, but the regional average will be weighed down by sluggish growth in some key economies, such as South Africa.

The funding squeeze will also impact the region's longer-term outlook. A shortage of funding may force countries to reduce resources for critical development sectors like health, education, and infrastructure, weakening the region's growth potential.

Four policy priorities can help address the macroeconomic imbalances in the context of current financing constraints:

- Consolidating public finances and strengthening public financial management amid difficult funding conditions. This will rely on continued revenue mobilization, better management of fiscal risks, and more proactive debt management. International assistance remains also critical to alleviating governments' financing constraints. For countries that require debt reprofiling or restructuring, a well-functioning debt-resolution framework is vital to creating fiscal space.

- Containing inflation. Monetary policy should be steered cautiously until inflation is firmly on a downward trajectory and projected to return to the central bank's target range.

- Allowing the exchange rate to adjust, while mitigating the adverse effects on the economy, including the rise in inflation and debt due to the currency depreciations.

- Ensuring that important efforts to fund and address climate change do not crowd out basic needs, like health and education. Climate finance provided by the international community must come on top of current aid flows.

Regional Economic Outlook Notes. A separate series of analytical notes are provided on topics of current interest. "Geo-Economic Fragmentation: Sub-Saharan Africa Caught Between the Fault Lines" demonstrates that sub-Saharan Africa stands to lose the most in a severely fragmented world, and stresses the need for building resilience. "Managing Exchange Rate Pressures in Sub-Saharan Africa: Adapting to New Realities" outlines the drivers and consequences of recent exchange-rate pressures and discusses policies to help soften the impact on the region's economies. "Closing the Gap: Concessional Climate Finance and Sub-Saharan Africa" considers the critical need for concessional finance in helping the region address climate change and explores ways in which additional flows might be unlocked.

The Big Funding Squeeze

The confluence of higher global interest rates, elevated sovereign debt spreads, and exchange rate depreciations, among other factors, has created a funding squeeze for many countries in sub-Saharan Africa. This challenge comes on top of policy struggles from the ramifications of the COVID-19 pandemic and the cost-of-living crisis. Reflecting these considerations, economic activity in the region will remain subdued in 2023, with growth at 3.6 percent before rebounding to 4.2 percent in 2024 predicated on a global recovery, subsiding inflation, and the winding down of monetary policy tightening.

Sub-Saharan Africa facing funding squeeze

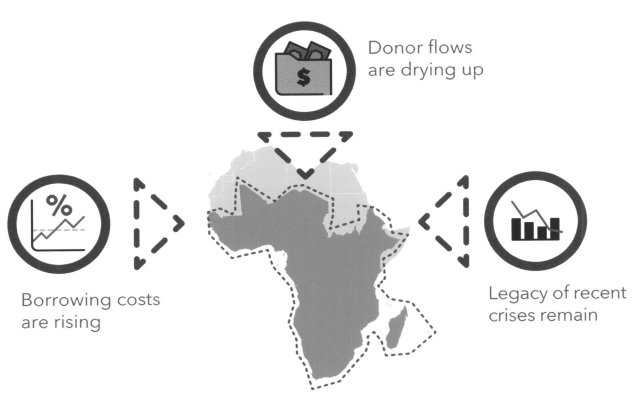

Donor flows are drying up

Borrowing costs are rising

Legacy of recent crises remain

Recent Developments: The Makings of a Funding Crisis[1]

Conjunctural factors have aggravated sub-Saharan Africa's already difficult financing situation...

The region's financing options have deteriorated significantly over the past year. The acceleration in the tightening of global monetary policy, prompted by the rapid pickup in global inflation after the onset of Russia's war in Ukraine, has led to higher interest rates worldwide and raised borrowing costs for sub-Saharan African countries, both on domestic and international markets.

Sovereign spreads for sub-Saharan Africa have soared (Figure 1)—to three times the emerging market average since the start of the global tightening cycle. Higher interest rates on US treasury bonds and the search for safe assets amid global uncertainty pushed the US dollar effective exchange rate to a 20-year high in 2022, increasing the value of dollar-denominated debt and dollar-denominated interest payments. Together, these factors have added to the region's external borrowing costs.

Higher uncertainty amid the pandemic and the war in Ukraine has also led to risk repricing, disproportionately affecting sub-Saharan African countries because of lower credit ratings, and cutting off virtually all frontier markets from international market access since spring 2022.[2] More specifically, Eurobond issuances for the region declined from $14 billion in 2021 to $6 billion in the first quarter of 2022.

Figure 1. Sub-Saharan Africa: Sovereign Spreads, 2021-23

(Basis points, simple average)

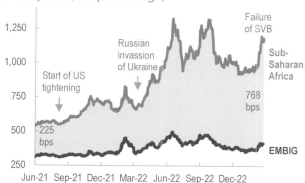

Source: Bloomberg Finance, L.P.
Note: Sub-Saharan Africa includes Angola, Côte d'Ivoire, Ethiopia, Gabon, Ghana, Kenya, Mozambique, Namibia, Nigeria, Senegal, South Africa. EMBIG = Emerging Market Bond Index Global.

The effect has been a drastic and pro-cyclical tightening of financing conditions, which has aggravated underlying vulnerabilities. Borrowing costs have increased significantly over the past decade, with interest payments as a share of revenue doubling over the same period. At 11 percent of revenues (excluding grants) for the median sub-Saharan African country in 2022, interest payments are about triple those of the median advanced economy (Figure 2). Structural shifts behind this increase in borrowing costs include a decline in aid budgets to the region that led some countries to turn to market-based finance, which is more expensive (Figure 3). Increased integration in international debt markets and deepening of domestic financial markets also made it easier to contract more private domestic and external debt on non-concessional terms. Finally, inflows from China, for a while a significant source of financing, have declined markedly more recently.

...on top of the fallout from multi-year shocks...

The financing squeeze comes at a most unfortunate time, as the region is facing elevated economic imbalances. In the wake of the COVID-19 pandemic and the war in Ukraine, macroeconomic imbalances have returned as a first order challenge for most African countries, and they are pushing countries close to the edge (Selassie 2022).

Inflation remains elevated and volatile. The median inflation rate in the region was about 10 percent in February 2023—more than double since the beginning of the pandemic. Besides registering double-digit headline inflation in roughly half of the countries in the region, about 80 percent are also experiencing double-digit food

---

[1] For more discussion on the origin of the financing crisis in sub-Saharan Africa, see also Selassie 2023.

[2] Although frontier markets represent only one-third of the countries, they account for 60 percent of the region's GDP and 60 percent of the total population.

Figure 2. Sub-Saharan Africa: Interest Payments to Revenue, Excluding Grants
(Percent, median)

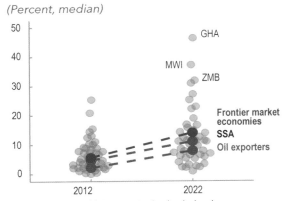

Source: IMF, World Economic Outlook database.
Note: See pages vi-vii for country acronyms and groupings.

Figure 3. Sub-Saharan Africa: Sources of Financing
(Percent of regional GDP)

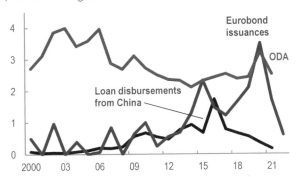

Sources: Bloomberg Finance, L.P. ; Organisation for Economic Co-operation and Development, OECD.stat; and World Bank, *International Debt Statistics.*
Note: ODA = Official Development Aid.

inflation in February. However, fuel price pressures have decelerated recently because international prices fell from their peak in mid-2022 by up to 30 percent as of the end of 2022, providing some reprieve for the region. About half of the countries have now reported a deceleration in inflation in recent months, but there were also resurgences; and because subsidies on fuel and food prices are being phased out this year (Cameroon, Central African Republic, Ethiopia, Senegal), inflation will likely remain volatile throughout 2023. A few countries also faced pressures to raise public wages in the second half of 2022 because of increases in the cost of living, triggered by higher food and fuel prices (Cameroon, Mali, Rwanda, The Gambia).

Public debt as a share of GDP is relatively high. Sub-Saharan Africa's public debt ratio—at 56 percent of GDP in 2022—has reached levels last seen in the early 2000s. Since the pandemic, the debt increase has been driven by widening fiscal deficits because of overlapping crises, slower growth, and exchange rate depreciations. Elevated public debt levels have raised concerns about debt sustainability, with 19 of the region's 35 low-income countries already in debt distress or facing high risk of debt distress in 2022—the same situation reported in the October 2022 *Regional Economic Outlook: Sub-Saharan Africa.*

Most currencies in the region depreciated against the US dollar in 2022. For those already grappling with high inflation, the weakening of the currency relative to the dollar made matters even worse because the region is highly dependent on imports with a significant share of them invoiced in dollars. Currency depreciations also contributed to higher general government debt because about 40 percent of sub-Saharan Africa's debt is external as of 2021. Although exchange rate pressures have eased since November 2022—in some cases because significant depreciations have already taken place—they remain elevated and volatile.

…resulting in another year of disrupted recovery…

Given this challenging environment, the region's growth will decline to 3.6 percent in 2023 from 3.9 percent in 2022 following the strong rebound of 2021. This subdued outlook in sub-Saharan Africa marks a growth slowdown, the second year in a row. Some common factors explain the growth underperformance, including the rise in central bank rates to fight inflation and the war in Ukraine dampening global economic activity and thus, export demand for the region. Nonetheless there are large variations across the region (Figure 4). Niger, the Democratic Republic of the Congo, and Senegal are on the higher end of the region's growth distribution, with this year's coming online of oil and gas in those countries expected to contribute significantly to higher GDP growth. On the opposite end, the significant economic contraction in Equatorial Guinea is a result of a decline in oil production. Meanwhile, South Africa's growth is projected to decelerate sharply to 0.1 percent in 2023, weighed down by an intensification of power outages, a weaker external environment, and a negative carry-over effect from the growth slowdown at the end of 2022.

Figure 4. Sub-Saharan Africa: Real GDP Growth, 2023
(Percent, fragile countries in red)

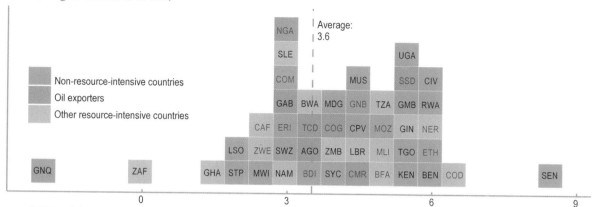

Source: IMF, World Economic Outlook database.
Note: See pages vi-vii for country acronyms and groupings.

The region's financial sector has held up relatively well. The share of non-performing loans has improved slightly—down to about 7½ percent in 2022 from nearly 9 percent of total loans for the median country in 2021. After a temporary decline during the pandemic, bank profitability has bounced back to the pre-COVID-19 trend as of mid-2022. However, the capital adequacy of banks in the region has dipped slightly in the last two years relative to its pre-pandemic peak in 2019.

…and undermining economic and development prospects.

Unlike many major advanced economies, countries in sub-Saharan Africa had limited fiscal space entering the pandemic recession, hampering policymakers' ability to mount an effective response. This has resulted in larger scarring effects on the economy, including from disruptions to education. The current funding squeeze is constraining many countries' ability to address these scars, contributing to the muted recovery. Moreover, authorities are forced to reduce resources for critical development sectors such as health, education, and infrastructure, weakening the region's medium-term growth prospects. Partly for these reasons, the catch-up in growth has remained elusive, with GDP per capita remaining stubbornly below pre-pandemic trend (Figure 5).

Figure 5. Real GDP per Capita, 2019–24
(2019 = 100, dashed line indicates pre-crisis trend)

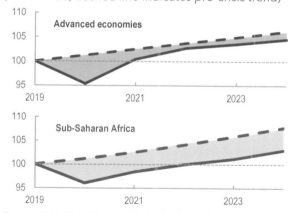

Source: IMF, World Economic Outlook database.

The lack of fiscal space has also made it challenging for countries to address the vast social needs, especially those in the most vulnerable segments of the population. Insufficient funding meant that the authorities struggled to scale up targeted support when the region faced record-high food, fuel, and fertilizer prices in 2022. In fact, the cost-of-living crisis remains a major concern for sub-Saharan Africa given the high incidence of poverty—35 percent of the population in sub-Saharan Africa was estimated to live under $2.15 a day as of 2019 (latest available data from the World Bank Low-Income Dataset). About 132 million people were estimated to be acutely food-insecure in 2022, an upward revision from the estimate of 123 million in the October 2022 *Regional Economic Outlook: Sub-Saharan Africa*.

The Outlook for a Two-speed Recovery in 2024

Consistent with the global rebound, regional growth will pick up from 3.6 percent to 4.2 percent in 2024…

Sub-Saharan Africa is poised to grow at 4.2 percent in 2024 from 3.6 percent in 2023. Almost four-fifths of the countries are projected to register a growth pickup in 2024, driven by higher private consumption and investment. Importantly, the recovery for sub-Saharan Africa is linked intricately to global developments that are conditional on the realization of three key global factors:

- Global economic activity is assumed to continue to recover from the effects of the war in Ukraine. This would translate into tailwinds for exporters in the region, while the dissipation of supply chain bottlenecks will ease import prices.

- Global inflation is projected to recede further in 2024. Thus, it is assumed that major central banks may slow the pace of monetary policy tightening in the second half of 2023 as inflation (excluding volatile food and energy prices) has been declining at a three-month rate—although at a slower pace than headline inflation—in most (though not all) major economies since mid-2022. Subsequently, a slower pace of tightening implies less pressure on exchange rates and spreads for the region. However, global interest rates are expected to remain elevated and well above pre-pandemic levels.

- Crude oil prices are expected to continue to fall by about 6 percent in 2024 relative to the previous year as demand pressures subside. Because net fuel importers represent two-thirds of the region's GDP, lower prices should affect sub-Saharan Africa's growth positively. Nonfuel commodity prices are projected to remain broadly unchanged.

Of course, there is large heterogeneity in growth across subgroups. The growth rebound is expected to be primarily driven by the non-resource-intensive and other resource-intensive countries (Figure 6). The former are projected to grow by 6.2 percent in 2024, following 5.7 percent in 2023, reflecting more dynamic and resilient economies—including those in the Eastern African Community—and aided by the recovery in non-mining activities including agriculture. Other (non-oil) resource-intensive countries are also projected to post strong rebounds, in some cases boosted by new mining projects (iron ore in Liberia and Sierra Leone; renewable energy commodities in the Democratic Republic of the Congo and Mali). In South Africa, activity is expected to recover in 2024 as the energy crisis abates and the external environment improves. However, growth among oil exporters is projected to decelerate in 2024 to 3.1 percent from 3.3 percent in 2023, mostly because of the continued decline in crude oil prices and production slowdowns. Nigeria's growth is forecast to decline to 3.0 percent next year.

Figure 6. Sub-Saharan Africa: Real GDP Growth, 2022–24
(Percent)

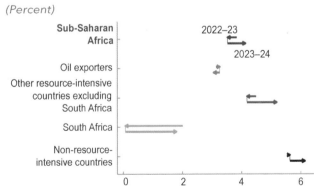

Source: IMF, World Economic Outlook database.
Note: See pages vi for country groupings.

Consistent with the expected receding of global inflation, the median inflation for the region is projected to be down at 5 percent by the end of 2024 (year-over-year), still above pre-pandemic levels but half that at the end of 2022. Sub-Saharan Africa is a large importer of food and energy items, which average 50 percent of the region's consumption basket. Thus, the recent onset in the decline in global food and fuel prices that is projected to continue throughout this year and next, is expected to contribute much to the slowdown in regional headline inflation.

…but faces significant downside risks.

The outlook for the global economy is clouded by sizable uncertainty because of the multiple shocks in recent years and ongoing financial sector turmoil. Compared to the January 2023 *World Economic Outlook Update*, global recession risks have increased, while concerns about stubbornly high inflation persist. Thus, global risks are squarely to the downside (April 2023 *World Economic Outlook*).

The ongoing banking sector turbulence in major economies could impact the region through several channels. A deterioration of business and consumer confidence could depress activity in the key advanced economies and spill over to African countries through lower demand for imports and lower commodity prices. In addition, while financial conditions in sub-Saharan African countries are not closely correlated with those in the United States or Europe, banking sector stress in the latter economies could nonetheless increase global risk aversion, which would aggravate the funding squeeze even further for the region. As in past episodes of global financial stress, a broad-based outflow of capital from emerging market and developing economies could occur, causing further dollar appreciation, which would worsen vulnerabilities in countries with large dollar-denominated external debt. The dollar appreciation would further depress global trade due to many products being invoiced in dollars.

Apart from risks in the banking sector, three additional types of global downside risks are worth highlighting. First, stickier-than-expected inflation could prompt further monetary policy tightening. This could lower net financial inflows to sub-Saharan Africa and aggravate balance of payment pressures, which would lead to domestic currency depreciations and squeeze already tight financing conditions even further. Another global risk is an escalation of the war in Ukraine, which could perpetuate already elevated global uncertainty and raise food and energy prices, making the financing environment even more difficult. Finally, a worsening in geoeconomic fragmentation could have negative spillovers into sub-Saharan Africa, including rising trade barriers and higher food prices, because the region relies highly on commodity exports and is sensitive to global demand and price shocks (Analytical Note "Geoeconomic Fragmentation: Sub-Saharan Africa Caught Between the Fault Lines").

Under a global downside scenario that considers severe financial sector stress, global real GDP growth in 2023 could be 1.8 percentage points below baseline and 2024 growth could be lower by 1.4 percentage points (April 2023 *World Economic Outlook*). The overall effect on global output is about one fourth the size of the impact of the 2008–09 global financial crisis. The slowdown would be accompanied by a disinflationary impulse, including lower oil and gas prices. Global trade would decrease because of depressed global demand, increased uncertainty, and the rising value of the dollar. The cumulative cost to sub-Saharan Africa would amount to a loss of −1.9 percent of GDP over 2023–24, with oil exporters experiencing more losses (−2.5 percent) relative to other resource-intensive countries (−1.8 percent) and non-resource-intensive countries (−1.4 percent).

Four Main Policy Priorities

The global slowdown, higher interest rates, and a dramatic pickup in global inflation have pushed many countries closer to the edge. The following four priorities are centered around policy strategies that aim to help policymakers address macroeconomic imbalances in the context of severe financing constraints.

Fiscal policy amid tighter financial conditions

Policymakers in sub-Saharan Africa have to adapt to an environment with tighter financing conditions, which has two important implications for the conduct of fiscal policy. First, debt vulnerabilities (already elevated) are likely to worsen. With rising borrowing costs, countries may find it challenging to refinance their existing liabilities and rollover longer maturities. This could create liquidity problems, which may, over time, raise solvency questions in some cases. Second, policymakers will struggle to cover even the most essential expenses for basic services let alone securing financing for further progress toward the Sustainable Development Goals.

Figure 7. Sub-Saharan Africa: Eurobonds Repayments, 2023–25
(Billions of US dollars)

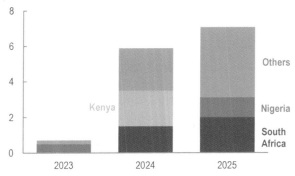

Source: Bloomberg Finance, L.P.

Figure 8. Sub-Saharan Africa: Debt Ratio at End-2022 and Fiscal Adjustment Needs
(Percent of GDP)

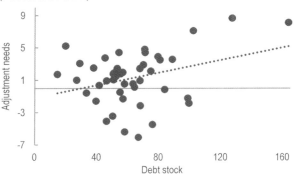

Sources: IMF, World Economic Outlook; and IMF staff calculations.
Note: Fiscal adjustment needs are computed as of 2023 in order to reduce debt ratio to 70 percent of GDP for countries above threshold within 6 years or stabilize at latest level for countries below threshold. Negative fiscal adjustment needs imply available fiscal space.

Looking ahead, the difficult funding environment for the region is likely to remain **and become a key feature of the new normal. Over the next few years, the region's countries are projected to have some of the world's highest interest bills relative to revenues, exceeding 50 percent in a few cases. In the next two years alone, a sizable share of outstanding Eurobond debt will come due—about $6 billion in 2024 and another $7 billion in 2025 (Figure 7). If countries struggle to make repayments or rollover debt, it could have potential repercussions on the region's economic growth and social development.**

In this context, consolidating public finances in the context of a credible and transparent medium-term fiscal policy framework **remains a priority for the region. As highlighted in the** <u>October 2022 *Regional Economic Outlook: Sub-Saharan Africa*</u>**, there is nonetheless heterogeneity among countries. Those that still have some fiscal space can use it to continue making much needed investments in human and physical capital to address development needs. But most countries with elevated debt vulnerabilities need to consolidate their public finances to preserve fiscal sustainability. For some, adjustment needs are moderate, but for others, adjustment needs are very large, and it is unlikely that fiscal consolidation alone will be enough to ensure fiscal sustainability (Figure 8). In this case, the necessary adjustment could be accompanied by debt reprofiling or restructuring.**

Countries have already started fiscal adjustment. **After a significant deterioration in 2020, the median fiscal deficit ratio in sub-Saharan Africa started to decline in 2021, with a consolidation of almost 1 percentage point of GDP projected for 2023. Fiscal consolidation, which is expected to continue into the medium term,** can be pursued in a way that minimizes possible negative impacts on growth and poverty. **This will require increased efforts to boost revenue mobilization, but also prioritizing and increasing the efficiency of spending where possible including the phasing out of untargeted fuel subsidies. Crucially, fiscal adjustment should make allowances for continuing social spending and protecting the most vulnerable populations amid the ongoing cost-of-living crisis. This can be done through targeted transfers to those particularly exposed to higher energy and food prices or an expansion of existing social safety nets. Saving part of the windfalls from higher commodity prices will be especially helpful for commodity exporters with elevated fiscal vulnerabilities.**

Beyond fiscal consolidation, authorities can take additional steps **to adapt to a world of tighter financing constraints:**

- Managing fiscal risks **resulting from the funding squeeze will be critical to improve fiscal sustainability. Given tighter budgets, the risk of fiscal slippage rises along with the temptation for governments to accumulate arrears, increase off-budget spending, extend guarantees and contingent liabilities. All these operations can** translate into so-called "stock-flow adjustments"[3], which have contributed significantly to the debt increase in the past decade (Figure 9). Containing these flows through better public financial management practices and better risk management is essential to improve debt dynamics, including by strengthening fiscal transparency and oversight of state-owned enterprises.

- By reinvigorating efforts to boost domestic revenue mobilization, countries can generate more resources for development spending, and attract more financing because a country's revenue stream is a main metric for its debt repayment capacity. Sub-Saharan African countries lag significantly in revenue collections, with a median tax ratio of only 13 percent of GDP in 2022, compared with 18 percent in other emerging economies and developing countries and 27 percent in advanced economies. Successful revenue mobilization efforts often require pursuing revenue administration reforms and improving the design of tax policies, including by expanding the base for value added tax and leveraging digitalization in tax collection (Togo, Guinea-Bissau).

- Effective and proactive debt management is critical to lowering debt risks. Debt management can help strike the balance between funding the government's needs and ensuring that debt levels remain sustainable. This includes enhancing debt reporting, lengthening maturities, and avoiding bunching of repayments to mitigate refinancing risks.

- For some countries that are likely to experience aggravated debt vulnerabilities and require debt reprofiling or restructuring, a well-functioning debt-resolution framework is vital to creating fiscal space. As the variety of debt instruments has widened, the creditor base has also become more diversified and negotiations more complex. Four countries in sub-Saharan Africa are currently seeking or are in the process of restructuring their debt under the Common Framework—Ghana is the latest in the group (others are Chad, Ethiopia, and Zambia). The Common Framework constitutes a step toward finding an effective and consistent way for the Group of Twenty and Paris Club official creditors to provide debt treatment for low-income countries, in case of need. Thus far, coordination among creditors has been challenging and the process has been slower than anticipated. Potential reforms include defining processes that are more predictable and timelier, earlier sharing of information between creditors and the international financial institutions, and introducing a standstill on debt service during the debt treatment process after staff-level agreement on an IMF program has been reached.

Finally, international assistance remains critical to alleviating governments' financing constraints. Donor nations should ensure that official development assistance continues to go to those countries in greatest need. Many fragile and conflict-affected states, for instance, still rely primarily on official development assistance for financing their development needs. Donors can work with recipient countries towards setting a more modest and well-defined set of objectives, such as public health initiatives or targeted capacity building, where smaller, more focused interventions can make a difference. In addition, higher volumes of countercyclical financing, particularly from International Financial Institutions (IFIs), are necessary to offset the highly procyclical nature of private capital flows. Countercyclical financing helps countries that have lost market access or are subject to capital outflows to smooth the adjustment, and, for instance, avoid abrupt and disruptive spending cuts.

Figure 9. Sub-Saharan Africa: Drivers of Changes in Public Debt Ratio between End-2012 and End-2022
(Cumulative change, percentage points of GDP)

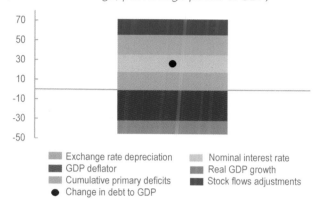

Legend:
- Exchange rate depreciation
- GDP deflator
- Cumulative primary deficits
- Change in debt to GDP
- Nominal interest rate
- Real GDP growth
- Stock flows adjustments

Sources: IMF, World Economic Outlook database; and IMF staff calculations.

---

[3] Stock-flow adjustments refer to discrepancies between the annual change in public debt and the budget deficit, a prominent feature of debt dynamics in many sub-Saharan African countries. In such a case, the fiscal deficit may not be a good depiction of financing needs as debt may increase more (or less) than the fiscal deficit. A positive stock-flow adjustment means that the increase in government debt exceeds the annual deficit (or decreases less than implied by the surplus).

Monetary policy amid high inflation

By the beginning of 2023, inflation had started to fall in about half of countries in sub-Saharan Africa, while inflation is still rising or very volatile for the rest. Regardless of the trajectory, inflation remains high, with at least 20 out of 45 countries still facing double-digit inflation, and a median inflation of about 10 percent as of February 2023, more than twice the level at the end of 2019 (Figure 10). Median core inflation, which excludes energy and basic food prices, was more than 6 percent as of the end of February (where data were available) but remains volatile, showing no clear signs of decline. Projections point to inflation staying above pre-pandemic levels throughout 2027. Thus, policymakers have to continue this delicate dance between keeping inflation in check while being mindful of the still-fragile recovery. The good news is that external factors (such as imported food and energy or swings in the exchange rate) rather than domestic demand pressures have driven much of the inflation in the region. Many of these external factors have subsided in recent months, and thus inflation is likely to follow suit, but because the transmission of lower international prices into domestic markets will take time, inflation is expected to remain above pre-pandemic levels in the near term.

Almost all central banks in the region have hiked policy rates since December 2021,[4] with cumulative rate hikes larger in countries with higher inflation. However, the median interest rate hike was only about 270 basis points in sub-Saharan Africa between end-2021 and February 2023—lower by almost 130 basis points compared with the median in emerging market and developing economies outside the region (Figure 11). For most countries, current policy rates remain well below average policy rates over the past decade, while short-term real rates in the region are also still broadly in negative territory. In some countries, growth in reserve money continues to exceed nominal GDP growth (Nigeria, Malawi). Angola is the only country to have cut the policy rate in early 2023, given the sharp decline in headline inflation.

Figure 10. Sub-Saharan Africa: Median Inflation, December 2021–February 2023

(Percent, year-over-year)

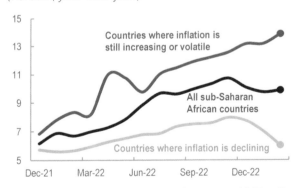

Sources: Haver Analytics; country authorities; and IMF staff calculations.
Note: Country groupings are based on recent evolution of inflation for the last 3 months. The sample includes 37 countries with available data.

Figure 11. Sub-Saharan Africa: Changes in Policy Rate and Inflation

(Percentage points, between December 2021 and February 2023)

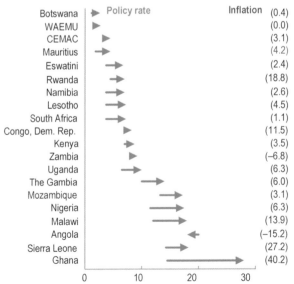

Sources: Haver Analytics; and IMF, *International Financial Statistics*.
Note: Numbers indicate change in inflation.

---

[4] Rates have stayed flat in a few countries like the Democratic Republic of the Congo and the Seychelles as of the end of February 2023.

What is needed to move ahead? Policymakers need to adjust the pace of monetary policy tightening to both the level and trajectory of inflation, in close coordination with fiscal policy, which can also tame domestic demand pressures where they exist and contain money growth:

- In cases where countries are still experiencing very high inflation, continued acceleration, or significant volatility, authorities need to continue to tighten policy rates decisively because these countries are susceptible to second-round effects and de-anchoring of inflation expectations. Tackling both after they become entrenched will be very difficult.

- In countries that have signs of inflation peaking, but where inflation is still relatively elevated, authorities need to steer monetary policy cautiously until inflation is firmly on a downward trajectory, and inflation projections return within the target band of the central bank in the medium term.

More generally, given the uncertainty in predicting turning points in the inflation trajectories, monetary policy needs to be data-dependent based on country-specific economic developments, including paying particular attention to wage growth in the coming months, but also international food and energy price developments because food and energy make up 50 percent of the region's consumption basket on average.

Countries with pegs or heavily managed floats have generally experienced lower inflation than those without pegs, but their currency arrangement constrains their ability to control the pace of monetary policy tightening. Anchor currencies in the region include the euro (West African Economic and Monetary Union and Central African Economic and Monetary Community), the South African rand, and the US dollar—all subject to a different pace of monetary policy tightening by their respective central banks. Thus, currency peggers will not only have to keep a close watch on elevated inflation and its trajectory but also keep policy rates in lock with the anchor policy rate to preserve external stability and foreign exchange reserves.

Exchange rate management amid large depreciation pressures

Sub-Saharan African countries experienced significant exchange rate depreciations in 2022 (Figure 12), exacerbating the financing crisis by increasing the external debt service burden. These pressures were predominantly brought on by shifts in global fundamentals, including increases in interest rates in advanced economies and adverse terms of trade. Currency depreciations contributed to a rise in inflation and public debt while deteriorating the trade balance in the near-term. Exchange rate pressures also manifested in the depletion of reserve assets—about a quarter of countries had reserves below three months of imports at the end of 2022—because foreign exchange inflows slowed down and central banks used their reserves to finance imports (Analytical Note "Managing Exchange Rate Pressures—Adapting to New Realities").

Figure 12. Sub-Saharan Africa: Exchange Rate versus US Dollar

(Percent change from September 2021 to February 2023. Asterisk = Peg)

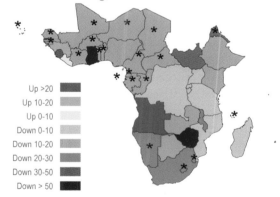

Up >20
Up 10-20
Up 0-10
Down 0-10
Down 10-20
Down 20-30
Down 30-50
Down > 50

Source: Bloomberg Finance, L.P.

Many countries acted to contain these pressures in 2022. The tightening of monetary policy helped to support their currencies, and some countries also intervened in foreign exchange markets to resist exchange rate pressures. As reserves dwindled over the course of 2022, the degree of intervention also slowed down. Many countries also applied administrative measures to control foreign exchange flows in 2022, including multiple currency practices (Nigeria), price control through moral suasion, and banning foreign currency transactions for local businesses. Some countries also resorted to unconventional measures such as buying oil with gold (Ghana), and foreign exchange rationing became even more acute in 2022 (Ethiopia, Nigeria).

Nonetheless, some adjustment of currencies seems unavoidable in many cases. There are certainly some reasons for sub-Saharan African countries to resist exchange rate pressures, including an elevated share of foreign-currency debt and weakly anchored inflation. But countries have to adjust to new fundamentals of higher global interest rates and tighter financing conditions that are expected to last into the foreseeable future. For most countries, the low levels of reserves limit the scope for interventions.

Policymakers can take several steps to mitigate possible adverse impacts on the economy as a result of the necessary currency adjustments. In countries where inflation is aggravated by the exchange rate passthrough, tighter monetary policy will help alleviate the pressure by keeping inflation expectations in check and stem capital outflows while attracting inflows. Where fiscal imbalances are key drivers of exchange rate pressures, fiscal consolidation can help to rein in external imbalances and contain the increase in debt related to currency depreciation.

In some cases, for countries that have sufficient reserve buffers, the use of foreign exchange intervention can reduce the volatility of exchange rate. For instance, for those with shallow foreign exchange markets, weak monetary policy credibility, and large foreign exchange mismatches, foreign exchange intervention can temporarily reduce some of the costs associated with excessive exchange rate movements. However, countries can easily run out of reserves if exchange rate pressures persist because of fundamental forces.

Responding to climate change without sacrificing basic needs

Critical development needs, like schooling, health, and infrastructure services, are in danger of not being adequately filled under the funding squeeze. Most governments have limited fiscal space, hampering their ability to protect the most vulnerable and allocate sufficient funds to essential development sectors. Limited financing makes it particularly challenging to address the ongoing food security crisis that is affecting the region.

If the difficulties in addressing basic needs were not enough already, climate change is presenting additional spending pressures on shrinking fiscal budgets. For instance, cyclone Freddy—one of the latest in a series of climate shocks to the region—has battered vulnerable families and communities in southern Africa, but countries have limited means for climate adaptation. For the African continent alone, adaptation costs could reach $50 billion per year by 2050, in a 2-degree Celsius scenario (GCA 2021), and mitigation costs for a clean energy transition in Africa have been estimated at around $190 billion per year until 2030 (IEA 2022). However, climate funding to the region remains well below these needs, with private and public sources estimated at about $22 billion in 2020, as shown in Figure 13 (Analytical Note "Closing the Gap: Concessional Climate Finance and Sub-Saharan Africa"). Advanced economies have also fallen far short of a 2009 pledge to mobilize $100 billion a year for climate actions in developing countries.

Figure 13. Climate Finance Flows to Sub-Saharan Africa, 2020

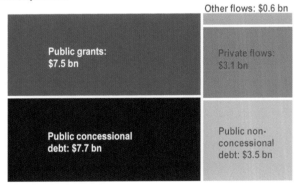

Source: Climate Policy Initiative.

It is important that resources allocated towards climate change do not crowd out those devoted to basic needs and other development goals. Official development assistance, for instance, has been declining over the last two decades, and despite a temporary surge during the COVID-19 pandemic, aid flows are likely to shrink further over the near term. More support from advanced economies is needed to ensure that the essential development needs of African countries are adequately financed, with the objective of fostering strong, resilient, and inclusive growth. Furthermore, climate finance must come on top of current aid flows rather than replacing them.

Therefore, what can be done to mobilize the additional climate financing to the region?

- Unlock more concessional finance. Sub-Saharan African countries encounter challenges in accessing concessional climate finance, in part because requirements vary greatly across financing providers. For example, climate funds—a key channel for concessional financing—have the potential to be scaled up significantly to help meet the region's climate adaptation and mitigation needs. However, the numerous access requirements and project selection criteria for these funds present serious hurdles for countries in the region seeking to access this financing. To help unlock concessional financing, development partners—including the IMF—can support countries in building and strengthening capacity. Priority areas include governance and public financial management, development of adequate data and climate strategies, formulation of legal and regulatory frameworks, and financial system reforms.

- Increase private climate finance. The private sector has the potential to mobilize significant climate finance in the region as it does in the rest of the world. This can be done by developing the use of financing instruments like green bonds or sustainability-linked bonds and attracting private institutional investors. Increasing the attractiveness of private climate finance will require better data to support financial risk monitoring and analysis on performance indicators, but also more transparency and disclosure.

- Join forces: leverage concessional finance to catalyze private finance. In many cases, the risk-adjusted returns of climate projects in the region are insufficiently attractive to international or domestic investors. Concessional finance in the form of guarantees, loan tenure extension, below market pricing and subordinated loans can help reduce the risks associated with climate projects and raise their attractiveness to private investors. This "crowding in" of private sector finance could increase the scale of climate infrastructure projects, although private funding is a difficult and complex issue, where options and best practices are still being developed.

The IMF's new Resilience and Sustainability Facility is an important new financing instrument that will help sub-Saharan Africa address longer-term structural challenges, including those posed by climate change. It was launched in 2022, and five countries are already benefiting from the facility, including one from sub-Saharan Africa (Rwanda). The Resilience and Sustainability Facility provides financing to support both adaptation and mitigation efforts, while also providing a framework of transparency, credibility, and stability that are essential in incentivizing private sector investments in climate resilient infrastructure and renewable energy projects.

Conclusion

Policymakers in sub-Saharan Africa are looking at yet at another difficult year, facing tighter financing conditions on top of the ongoing repercussions from a recent cascading series of shocks. Despite serious financing constraints, there are still a few policy levers available to alleviate the situation. For instance, domestic revenue mobilization offers a potential source of financing. Moreover, improving domestic legal and regulatory frameworks and undertaking financial systems reforms would not only attract much needed climate finance but also other types of private finance to the region that can help address basic needs and development goals in addition to those arising from climate change. Above all, sub-Saharan Africa will require international assistance in addressing the funding squeeze. The IMF also stands ready to support the region. As of March 2023, the IMF has lending arrangements with 21 countries in the region and has received many program requests. The disbursements associated with IMF programs, emergency financing facilities, and the special drawing rights allocation represented $50 billion between 2020 and 2022.

References

Global Center on Adaptation (GCA). 2021. *State and Trends in Adaptation Report 2021. How Adaptation Can Make Africa Safer, Greener and More Prosperous in a Warming World.* https://gca.org/wp-content/uploads/2022/08/GCA_STA_2021_Complete_website.pdf

International Energy Agency (IEA). 2022. "Africa Energy Outlook 2022." *World Energy Outlook Report.* International Energy Agency, Paris.

Selassie, Abebe Aemro. 2022. "The Return of Macroeconomic Imbalances: Adapting to Life on the Edge." Remarks at the 13th Andrew Crockett Lecture Governors' Roundtable for African Central Bankers, All Souls College, Oxford. https://www.imf.org/en/News/Articles/2022/06/27/sp062722-13th-andrew-crockett-lecture-governors-roundtable-for-african-central-bankers.

Selassie, Abebe Aemro. 2023. Remarks at the 2023 Oxford Center for the Study of African Economies Conference, St Catherine's College, Oxford. https://www.imf.org/en/News/Articles/2023/03/20/sp032023-abebe-selassie-2023-oxford-csae-conference.

Statistical Appendix

Unless otherwise noted, data and projections presented in this Regional Economic Outlook are IMF staff estimates as of March 30, 2023, consistent with the projections underlying the April 2023 *World Economic Outlook*.

The data and projections cover 45 sub-Saharan African countries in the IMF's African Department. Data definitions follow established international statistical methodologies to the extent possible. However, in some cases, data limitations limit comparability across countries.

Country Groupings

- Countries are aggregated into three (nonoverlapping) groups: oil exporters, other resource-intensive countries, and non-resource-intensive countries (see table on page vi for the country groupings).

- The oil exporters are countries where net oil exports make up 30 percent or more of total exports.

- The other resource-intensive countries are those where nonrenewable natural resources represent 25 percent or more of total exports.

- The non-resource-intensive countries refer to those that are not classified as either oil exporters or other resource-intensive countries.

- Countries are also aggregated into four (overlapping) groups: oil exporters, middle-income, low-income, and countries in fragile and conflict-affected situations. (see table on page vi for the country groupings).

- The membership of these groups reflects the most recent data on per capita gross national income (averaged over three years) and the World Bank, Classification of Fragile and Conflict-Affected Situations.

- The middle-income countries had per capita gross national income in the years 2019–21 of more than $1,085.00 (World Bank, using the Atlas method).

- The low-income countries had average per capita gross national income in the years 2019–21 equal to or lower than $1,085.00 (World Bank, Atlas method).

- The countries in fragile and conflict-affected situations are classified based on the World Bank, Classification of Fragile and Conflict-Affected Situations, FY2023.

- The membership of sub-Saharan African countries in the major regional cooperation bodies is shown on page vi: CFA franc zone, comprising the West African Economic and Monetary Union (WAEMU) and CEMAC; the Common Market for Eastern and Southern Africa (COMESA); the East Africa Community (EAC-5); the Economic Community of West African States (ECOWAS); the Southern African Development Community (SADC); and the Southern African Customs Union (SACU). EAC-5 aggregates include data for Rwanda and Burundi, which joined the group only in 2007.

Methods of Aggregation

- In Tables SA1 and SA3, country group composites for real GDP growth and broad money are calculated as the arithmetic average of data for individual countries, weighted by GDP valued at purchasing power parity as a share of total group GDP. The source of purchasing power parity weights is the World Economic Outlook (WEO) database.

- In Table SA1, country group composites for consumer prices are calculated as the geometric average of data for individual countries, weighted by GDP valued at purchasing power parity as a share of total group GDP. The source of purchasing power parity weights is the WEO database.

- In Tables SA2–SA4, country group composites, except for broad money, are calculated as the arithmetic average of data for individual countries, weighted by GDP in US dollars at market exchange rates as a share of total group GDP.

List of Sources and Footnotes for Statistical Appendix Tables SA1-SA4

Tables SA1.,SA3.

Sources: IMF, Common Surveillance database; and IMF, April 2023, World Economic Outlook database.

[1] In 2019 Zimbabwe authorities introduced the real-time gross settlement (RTGS) dollar, later renamed the Zimbabwe dollar, and are in the process of redenominating their national accounts statistics. Current data are subject to revision. The Zimbabwe dollar previously ceased circulating in 2009, and between 2009-19, Zimbabwe operated under a multicurrency regime with the US dollar as the unit of account.

Note: "..." denotes data not available.

Table SA2.

Sources: IMF, Common Surveillance database; and IMF, April 2023, World Economic Outlook database.

[1] For Zambia, government debt projections for 2022-24 are omitted due to ongoing debt restructuring.

[2] In 2019 Zimbabwe authorities introduced the real-time gross settlement (RTGS) dollar, later renamed the Zimbabwe dollar, and are in the process of redenominating their national accounts statistics. Current data are subject to revision. The Zimbabwe dollar previously ceased circulating in 2009, and between 2009-19, Zimbabwe operated under a multicurrency regime with the US dollar as the unit of account.

Note: "..." denotes data not available.

Table SA4.

Sources: IMF, Common Surveillance database; and IMF, April 2023, World Economic Outlook database.

[1] As a member of the West African Economic and Monetary Union (WAEMU), see WAEMU aggregate for reserves data.

[2] As a member of the Central African Economic and Monetary Community (CEMAC), see CEMAC aggregate for reserves data.

[3] For Zambia, external debt projections for 2022-24 are omitted due to ongoing debt restructuring.

[4] In 2019 Zimbabwe authorities introduced the real-time gross settlement (RTGS) dollar, later renamed the Zimbabwe dollar, and are in the process of redenominating their national accounts statistics. Current data are subject to revision. The Zimbabwe dollar previously ceased circulating in 2009, and between 2009-19, Zimbabwe operated under a multicurrency regime with the US dollar as the unit of account.

Note: "..." denotes data not available.

Table SA1. Real GDP Growth and Consumer Prices

	Real GDP (Annual percent change)						Consumer Prices, Annual Average (Annual percent change)					
	2011–19	2020	2021	2022	2023	2024	2011–19	2020	2021	2022	2023	2024
Angola	2.0	−5.6	1.1	2.8	3.5	3.7	16.3	22.3	25.8	21.4	11.7	10.8
Benin	5.1	3.8	7.2	6.0	6.0	5.9	1.2	3.0	1.7	1.5	3.0	2.0
Botswana	4.1	−8.7	11.8	6.4	3.7	4.3	4.6	1.9	6.7	12.2	6.5	5.2
Burkina Faso	5.7	1.9	6.9	2.5	4.9	5.9	1.0	1.9	3.9	14.1	1.5	2.3
Burundi	1.9	0.3	3.1	1.8	3.3	6.0	7.1	7.3	8.3	18.9	16.0	13.0
Cabo Verde	4.0	−14.8	7.0	10.5	4.4	5.4	1.1	0.6	1.9	7.9	4.5	2.0
Cameroon	4.4	0.5	3.6	3.4	4.3	4.4	1.9	2.5	2.3	5.3	5.9	4.7
Central African Republic	−0.7	1.0	1.0	0.4	2.5	3.8	4.9	0.9	4.3	5.8	6.3	2.7
Chad	2.4	−2.1	−1.1	2.5	3.5	3.7	1.9	4.5	−0.8	5.3	3.4	3.0
Comoros	3.1	−0.2	2.1	2.4	3.0	3.6	1.8	0.8	−0.0	12.0	8.1	1.4
Congo, Democratic Republic of the	5.9	1.7	6.2	6.6	6.3	6.5	10.2	11.4	9.0	9.0	10.8	7.2
Congo, Republic of	−0.5	−6.2	1.5	2.8	4.1	4.6	2.3	1.4	2.0	3.5	3.3	3.2
Côte d'Ivoire	6.5	1.7	7.0	6.7	6.2	6.6	1.5	2.4	4.2	5.2	3.7	1.8
Equatorial Guinea	−2.7	−4.2	−3.2	1.6	−1.8	−8.2	2.5	4.8	−0.1	5.0	5.7	5.2
Eritrea	4.6	−0.5	2.9	2.6	2.8	2.9	2.6	5.6	6.6	7.4	6.4	4.1
Eswatini	2.5	−1.6	7.9	0.5	2.8	2.5	5.9	3.9	3.7	4.8	5.4	4.8
Ethiopia	9.5	6.1	6.3	6.4	6.1	6.4	14.4	20.4	26.8	33.9	31.4	23.5
Gabon	3.7	−1.9	1.5	2.8	3.0	3.1	2.3	1.7	1.1	4.3	3.4	2.6
The Gambia	2.5	0.6	4.3	4.4	5.6	6.3	6.3	5.9	7.4	11.5	11.3	8.7
Ghana	6.5	0.5	5.4	3.2	1.6	2.9	11.8	9.9	10.0	31.9	45.4	22.2
Guinea	6.2	4.9	4.3	4.3	5.6	5.7	11.4	10.6	12.6	10.5	8.1	7.5
Guinea-Bissau	3.9	1.5	6.4	3.5	4.5	5.0	1.3	1.5	3.3	7.9	5.0	3.0
Kenya	4.7	−0.3	7.5	5.4	5.3	5.4	7.4	5.3	6.1	7.6	7.8	5.6
Lesotho	1.5	−3.9	2.1	2.1	2.2	2.3	5.1	5.0	6.0	8.2	6.8	5.5
Liberia	2.8	−3.0	5.0	4.8	4.3	5.5	12.5	17.0	7.8	7.6	6.9	5.9
Madagascar	3.2	−7.1	5.7	4.2	4.2	4.8	7.0	4.2	5.8	8.2	9.5	8.3
Malawi	4.1	0.9	4.6	0.8	2.4	3.2	17.2	8.6	9.3	20.8	24.7	18.3
Mali	4.3	−1.2	3.1	3.7	5.0	5.1	1.1	0.5	3.8	10.1	5.0	2.8
Mauritius	3.7	−14.6	3.5	8.3	4.6	4.1	3.0	2.5	4.0	10.8	9.5	6.9
Mozambique	5.5	−1.2	2.3	4.1	5.0	8.2	7.0	3.1	5.7	9.8	7.4	6.5
Namibia	2.8	−8.0	2.7	3.8	2.8	2.6	5.2	2.2	3.6	6.1	5.0	4.6
Niger	5.9	3.5	1.4	11.1	6.1	13.0	0.7	2.9	3.8	4.2	2.8	2.5
Nigeria	3.0	−1.8	3.6	3.3	3.2	3.0	11.6	13.2	17.0	18.8	20.1	15.8
Rwanda	7.1	−3.4	10.9	6.8	6.2	7.5	3.9	7.7	0.8	13.9	8.2	5.0
São Tomé & Príncipe	4.0	3.0	1.9	0.9	2.0	2.5	8.1	9.8	8.1	18.0	17.9	7.3
Senegal	5.0	1.3	6.1	4.7	8.3	10.6	1.0	2.5	2.2	9.7	5.0	2.0
Seychelles	4.7	−7.7	7.9	8.8	3.9	3.9	3.0	1.2	9.8	2.7	3.1	3.7
Sierra Leone	5.0	−2.0	4.1	2.8	3.1	4.8	10.0	13.4	11.9	27.2	37.8	25.9
South Africa	1.6	−6.3	4.9	2.0	0.1	1.8	5.3	3.3	4.6	6.9	5.8	4.8
South Sudan	−5.3	−6.5	5.3	6.6	5.6	4.6	98.6	24.0	30.2	17.6	27.8	10.0
Tanzania	6.7	4.8	4.9	4.7	5.2	6.2	7.3	3.3	3.7	4.4	4.9	4.3
Togo	5.7	1.8	5.3	5.4	5.5	5.5	1.4	1.8	4.5	7.6	5.3	2.9
Uganda	5.3	−1.3	6.0	4.9	5.7	5.7	6.8	2.8	2.2	6.8	7.6	6.4
Zambia	4.3	−2.8	4.6	3.4	4.0	4.1	9.0	15.7	22.0	11.0	8.9	7.7
Zimbabwe[1]	4.6	−7.8	8.5	3.0	2.5	2.6	30.2	557.2	98.5	193.4	172.2	134.6
Sub-Saharan Africa	**3.7**	**−1.7**	**4.8**	**3.9**	**3.6**	**4.2**	**8.3**	**10.1**	**11.0**	**14.5**	**14.0**	**10.5**
Median	4.4	−1.2	4.6	3.7	4.2	4.6	4.5	3.9	4.6	8.2	6.8	5.2
Excluding Nigeria and South Africa	5.0	0.0	5.2	4.8	4.8	5.4	8.0	11.1	10.7	15.2	14.1	10.1
Oil-exporting countries	**2.7**	**−2.3**	**3.0**	**3.2**	**3.3**	**3.1**	**11.2**	**13.0**	**15.9**	**17.2**	**16.8**	**13.4**
Excluding Nigeria	2.0	−3.6	1.5	2.9	3.4	3.3	10.2	12.3	13.2	13.0	8.5	7.4
Oil-importing countries	**4.4**	**−1.3**	**5.7**	**4.3**	**3.7**	**4.7**	**6.7**	**8.6**	**8.5**	**13.1**	**12.5**	**9.0**
Excluding South Africa	5.8	0.8	6.0	5.1	5.1	5.8	7.5	10.9	10.2	15.6	15.2	10.6
Middle-income countries	**3.1**	**−2.9**	**4.5**	**3.4**	**2.9**	**3.4**	**8.2**	**8.5**	**10.5**	**13.1**	**13.0**	**9.6**
Excluding Nigeria and South Africa	4.2	−1.7	5.0	4.4	4.3	4.7	7.4	7.9	9.1	12.5	11.7	7.6
Low-income countries	**6.0**	**1.9**	**5.4**	**5.1**	**5.4**	**6.1**	**8.8**	**14.8**	**12.5**	**18.2**	**16.7**	**12.9**
Excluding low-income countries in fragile and conflict-affected situations	5.6	1.0	5.6	4.5	5.1	5.7	7.8	4.9	4.8	8.2	8.5	6.9
Countries in fragile and conflict-affected situations	**4.1**	**−0.2**	**4.2**	**4.1**	**4.1**	**4.4**	**10.3**	**15.6**	**16.4**	**20.3**	**20.0**	**15.5**
CFA franc zone	4.4	0.6	4.5	4.8	5.2	5.9	1.6	2.4	2.8	6.4	4.1	2.7
CEMAC	2.4	−1.4	1.7	2.9	3.3	2.9	2.2	2.7	1.5	4.9	4.9	4.0
WAEMU	5.7	1.7	5.9	5.7	6.1	7.4	1.2	2.2	3.5	7.1	3.7	2.1
COMESA (SSA members)	5.8	0.5	6.5	5.4	5.3	5.6	9.4	17.1	14.6	19.4	18.5	14.1
EAC-5	5.5	0.9	6.6	5.1	5.4	5.8	7.1	4.4	4.4	7.0	7.0	5.4
ECOWAS	4.0	−0.6	4.4	3.9	3.8	4.2	9.3	10.2	12.7	17.0	17.9	12.6
SACU	1.8	−6.4	5.2	2.3	0.4	2.0	5.2	3.2	4.6	7.1	5.8	4.8
SADC	2.8	−4.4	4.6	3.2	2.3	3.4	7.7	10.7	9.6	11.5	9.6	8.0

See sources on page 16.

Table SA2. Overall Fiscal Balance, Including Grants and Government Debt

	Overall Fiscal Balance, Including Grants (Percent of GDP)						Government Debt (Percent of GDP)					
	2011–19	2020	2021	2022	2023	2024	2011–19	2020	2021	2022	2023	2024
Angola	−0.5	−1.9	3.8	1.6	−0.2	−1.9	59.8	138.9	86.9	67.0	63.3	59.2
Benin	−2.4	−4.7	−5.7	−5.6	−4.3	−2.9	30.1	46.1	50.3	52.4	52.8	51.6
Botswana	−0.9	−10.9	−2.4	−2.0	−2.7	−1.5	17.6	18.7	19.0	19.9	20.6	19.3
Burkina Faso	−3.3	−5.1	−7.4	−10.4	−7.8	−6.7	30.3	44.9	48.2	54.3	58.0	60.2
Burundi	−5.1	−6.3	−5.2	−12.1	−4.6	−2.7	45.1	66.0	66.6	68.3	69.5	61.0
Cabo Verde	−5.5	−9.1	−7.3	−4.5	−5.0	−3.6	111.0	145.1	142.9	127.4	120.2	117.9
Cameroon	−3.5	−3.2	−3.0	−1.8	−0.8	−0.6	27.6	44.9	46.8	46.4	42.8	40.4
Central African Republic	−1.3	−3.4	−6.0	−5.6	−3.0	−2.1	47.4	43.4	47.6	50.7	49.1	48.5
Chad	−0.9	2.1	−1.6	5.1	7.0	4.5	41.1	54.1	55.9	50.4	43.7	40.1
Comoros	0.5	−0.5	−2.8	−3.7	−6.4	−5.6	18.1	24.0	25.4	29.1	32.5	35.7
Congo, Democratic Republic of the	0.1	−1.4	−0.9	−1.6	−1.5	−2.5	18.0	16.7	16.3	14.6	11.0	9.0
Congo, Republic of	−2.1	−1.2	1.8	6.6	4.8	5.1	62.3	112.1	107.9	99.6	96.5	89.2
Côte d'Ivoire	−2.4	−5.4	−4.8	−6.7	−5.1	−4.0	32.4	46.3	50.9	56.8	63.3	60.6
Equatorial Guinea	−5.0	−1.7	2.6	4.7	3.3	1.7	25.2	48.4	42.6	27.1	26.4	29.5
Eritrea	−2.9	−4.4	−4.1	−1.3	−0.1	0.6	173.6	179.7	175.4	163.8	146.3	135.3
Eswatini	−4.5	−4.5	−4.6	−5.7	0.7	−0.8	22.5	41.2	41.5	45.4	39.3	37.2
Ethiopia	−2.3	−2.8	−2.8	−4.2	−3.5	−3.0	49.5	53.9	53.8	46.4	37.6	33.3
Gabon	0.5	−2.2	−1.9	1.8	0.9	0.3	44.5	78.3	65.8	55.1	60.3	58.2
The Gambia	−4.3	−2.2	−4.6	−4.8	−2.7	−2.1	70.2	85.9	83.5	84.0	73.0	68.6
Ghana	−6.6	−17.4	−12.1	−9.9	−7.3	−8.4	49.6	72.3	79.6	88.8	98.7	92.8
Guinea	0.6	−3.1	−1.7	−0.7	−2.3	−2.4	40.2	47.5	40.6	33.4	30.0	30.1
Guinea-Bissau	−2.9	−9.6	−5.6	−5.5	−3.8	−3.2	55.6	78.2	78.9	79.5	76.5	74.7
Kenya	−6.2	−8.1	−7.1	−6.0	−5.2	−4.4	46.7	67.8	67.0	67.9	66.6	65.4
Lesotho	−2.9	0.3	−4.4	−3.4	2.5	8.4	41.8	60.0	56.4	57.9	58.5	57.3
Liberia	−3.9	−3.8	−2.4	−6.9	−4.9	−3.9	28.7	58.7	53.3	55.4	57.1	56.1
Madagascar	−2.1	−4.0	−2.8	−6.8	−3.0	−3.3	38.1	51.2	52.3	57.0	53.1	52.0
Malawi	−3.8	−8.2	−8.6	−10.4	−7.8	−8.0	35.5	54.8	61.6	70.1	72.2	69.4
Mali	−2.7	−5.4	−4.8	−4.8	−4.8	−4.3	31.5	46.9	50.7	53.2	54.1	54.9
Mauritius	−3.3	−10.4	−4.0	−3.2	−4.2	−3.6	62.2	94.6	88.4	80.9	78.1	77.1
Mozambique	−4.4	−5.4	−3.6	−5.2	−4.8	−3.1	78.9	120.0	107.2	104.5	102.8	103.1
Namibia	−6.1	−8.1	−8.8	−7.3	−4.1	−2.7	38.6	66.6	72.0	71.3	68.5	66.8
Niger	−3.7	−4.8	−5.9	−6.9	−5.3	−4.1	28.2	45.0	51.3	51.1	52.5	49.4
Nigeria	−3.1	−5.4	−6.0	−5.5	−5.3	−5.4	21.9	34.5	36.5	38.0	38.8	39.0
Rwanda	−2.6	−9.5	−7.0	−6.5	−5.4	−6.1	33.0	65.6	66.6	64.4	67.1	71.1
São Tomé & Príncipe	−4.7	5.9	1.5	8.1	2.7	2.3	81.3	81.4	70.6	58.1	54.8	54.2
Senegal	−3.9	−6.4	−6.3	−6.1	−4.9	−4.0	47.2	69.2	73.2	75.0	73.1	69.9
Seychelles	1.5	−16.3	−5.5	−1.0	−2.0	−1.8	67.0	84.8	72.9	63.4	62.5	60.0
Sierra Leone	−5.1	−5.8	−7.3	−10.9	−6.2	−2.9	51.5	76.3	79.3	98.8	92.2	84.9
South Africa	−4.0	−9.6	−5.6	−4.5	−5.9	−6.1	45.0	69.0	69.0	71.0	72.3	74.0
South Sudan	−5.7	−5.6	−9.4	0.9	5.8	7.0	53.0	49.9	58.5	39.6	48.4	46.1
Tanzania	−2.7	−2.5	−3.4	−3.3	−2.9	−2.6	36.3	39.8	42.1	41.6	40.1	38.5
Togo	−3.9	−6.9	−4.6	−7.3	−6.1	−5.3	48.8	60.3	63.7	68.0	68.5	69.0
Uganda	−3.0	−7.5	−7.5	−5.8	−4.1	−3.3	27.8	46.3	50.6	50.8	50.2	49.2
Zambia[1]	−6.3	−13.8	−8.1	−7.9	−6.3	−6.7	50.9	140.2	110.8	...	...	...
Zimbabwe[2]	−3.4	0.8	−2.2	−2.1	−3.0	−2.2	51.8	84.4	59.8	92.8	102.3	100.0
Sub-Saharan Africa	**−3.3**	**−6.4**	**−5.0**	**−4.4**	**−4.3**	**−4.2**	**37.6**	**57.1**	**56.6**	**56.5**	**55.5**	**53.9**
Median	−3.1	−5.1	−4.6	−4.8	−4.1	−2.9	41.4	60.0	59.8	57.9	60.3	59.2
Excluding Nigeria and South Africa	−3.1	−5.7	−4.4	−4.0	−3.3	−3.1	42.6	63.3	60.1	59.2	57.0	53.9
Oil-exporting countries	**−2.6**	**−4.7**	**−4.1**	**−3.1**	**−3.4**	**−3.8**	**30.4**	**48.8**	**46.3**	**45.1**	**44.5**	**43.6**
Excluding Nigeria	−1.7	−2.1	0.5	1.6	0.8	−0.3	48.7	89.9	70.1	59.3	56.8	53.8
Oil-importing countries	**−3.8**	**−7.4**	**−5.5**	**−5.1**	**−4.8**	**−4.5**	**42.7**	**61.4**	**61.6**	**62.9**	**61.5**	**59.6**
Excluding South Africa	−3.6	−6.4	−5.4	−5.4	−4.3	−3.8	41.2	58.0	58.0	59.1	57.1	53.9
Middle-income countries	**−3.5**	**−7.4**	**−5.4**	**−4.5**	**−4.6**	**−4.8**	**37.2**	**59.1**	**58.6**	**58.7**	**58.8**	**57.9**
Excluding Nigeria and South Africa	−3.5	−7.6	−4.8	−3.8	−3.3	−3.3	45.1	74.3	68.4	66.7	66.6	63.7
Low-income countries	**−2.6**	**−3.6**	**−3.8**	**−4.2**	**−3.3**	**−3.0**	**39.4**	**51.2**	**50.5**	**50.5**	**46.9**	**43.8**
Excluding low-income countries in fragile and conflict-affected situations	−2.7	−4.9	−4.9	−4.9	−3.7	−3.4	35.5	48.0	50.0	50.1	48.3	47.0
Countries in fragile and conflict-affected situations	**−2.8**	**−4.4**	**−4.7**	**−4.4**	**−4.1**	**−4.0**	**28.8**	**42.7**	**43.4**	**44.1**	**42.6**	**41.0**
CFA franc zone	−2.7	−4.3	−4.0	−3.6	−2.8	−2.4	35.3	53.9	56.0	56.1	57.6	56.0
CEMAC	−2.5	−2.0	−1.5	1.5	1.5	1.0	36.8	59.9	58.1	51.9	50.3	48.3
WAEMU	−3.0	−5.5	−5.5	−6.7	−5.3	−4.3	34.7	50.5	54.8	58.7	61.7	60.1
COMESA (SSA members)	−3.5	−5.4	−4.7	−4.9	−3.9	−3.6	42.1	60.4	57.4	57.6	52.7	48.9
EAC-5	−4.3	−6.3	−6.1	−5.3	−4.3	−3.7	39.2	55.5	56.7	56.7	55.3	53.8
ECOWAS	−3.3	−6.7	−6.5	−6.1	−5.4	−5.2	27.7	43.2	46.6	48.4	49.8	48.7
SACU	−4.0	−9.5	−5.5	−4.5	−5.6	−5.7	43.5	66.5	66.7	68.5	69.4	70.8
SADC	−3.2	−7.0	−3.9	−3.4	−4.1	−4.3	45.1	70.4	64.4	64.5	63.4	62.4

See sources on page 16.

Table SA3. Broad Money and External Current Account, Including Grants

	Broad Money (Percent of GDP)						External Current Account, Including Grants (Percent of GDP)					
	2011–19	2020	2021	2022	2023	2024	2011–19	2020	2021	2022	2023	2024
Angola	34.6	38.4	24.4	19.5	19.3	19.2	3.0	1.5	11.2	11.0	6.2	3.1
Benin	28.1	30.5	32.6	32.6	32.6	32.6	−4.9	−1.7	−4.2	−5.7	−5.8	−5.0
Botswana	44.7	52.5	45.3	44.1	46.2	45.9	2.0	−8.7	−0.5	3.1	3.3	5.4
Burkina Faso	32.3	43.6	49.0	41.9	43.1	43.6	−5.1	4.1	−0.4	−5.2	−3.6	−2.7
Burundi	27.0	46.3	50.6	56.3	57.8	59.7	−14.1	−10.3	−12.4	−15.7	−15.6	−13.2
Cabo Verde	92.9	114.3	107.1	99.3	98.4	98.8	−6.9	−15.0	−11.3	−7.5	−5.0	−4.0
Cameroon	21.7	26.6	29.1	30.7	30.2	30.5	−3.3	−3.7	−4.0	−1.6	−2.8	−3.0
Central African Republic	24.0	30.3	33.3	31.9	29.6	28.9	−7.1	−8.2	−11.0	−13.3	−8.8	−7.4
Chad	14.6	20.8	23.3	21.3	21.2	20.4	−7.6	−7.3	−4.5	2.8	−1.4	−4.9
Comoros	25.1	31.2	36.7	36.7	35.0	33.5	−3.1	−1.7	0.8	−4.6	−7.3	−6.4
Congo, Democratic Republic of the	11.5	20.2	22.2	21.1	22.1	23.3	−4.4	−2.2	−0.9	−2.2	−3.9	−3.0
Congo, Republic of	27.4	35.8	34.0	31.8	36.8	38.3	−3.2	13.5	14.6	21.2	4.8	0.1
Côte d'Ivoire	10.9	13.5	15.2	14.5	13.6	13.3	−0.3	−3.1	−4.0	−6.5	−5.7	−5.3
Equatorial Guinea	13.2	17.1	14.7	10.4	10.4	10.4	−7.6	−4.2	−3.6	0.0	−2.1	−5.8
Eritrea	207.6	232.1	232.1	232.1	232.1	232.1	14.9	14.2	14.1	12.9	14.1	12.4
Eswatini	26.8	32.3	30.3	29.8	28.9	28.5	6.0	7.1	2.7	−1.7	3.4	3.5
Ethiopia	29.2	30.8	31.1	27.9	26.7	26.3	−7.1	−4.6	−3.2	−4.3	−3.4	−2.6
Gabon	23.7	27.9	23.1	21.9	24.6	26.6	2.4	−6.9	−4.5	1.2	−0.1	−1.1
The Gambia	38.6	56.0	59.5	55.3	52.6	51.2	−7.6	−3.0	−3.8	−15.0	−13.8	−10.5
Ghana	24.1	30.8	29.5	29.3	27.2	26.6	−5.5	−3.8	−3.7	−2.3	−2.9	−2.0
Guinea	24.2	27.6	25.7	27.9	24.4	24.9	−16.3	−16.1	−2.1	−6.2	−5.2	−4.6
Guinea-Bissau	38.5	45.6	50.6	48.4	47.1	46.7	−2.4	−2.6	−0.8	−5.9	−4.9	−4.7
Kenya	36.8	37.2	35.0	33.2	32.0	31.8	−6.9	−4.8	−5.2	−4.7	−5.3	−5.3
Lesotho	34.2	40.3	37.2	34.8	34.2	34.2	−6.1	−1.0	−4.4	−4.4	0.6	1.0
Liberia	20.2	25.5	24.6	25.0	25.1	25.2	−20.1	−16.4	−17.9	−15.7	−17.0	−18.3
Madagascar	23.4	28.7	28.6	34.3	35.0	36.0	−2.7	−5.4	−5.0	−5.6	−5.7	−5.1
Malawi	17.2	17.5	20.1	23.6	24.7	24.9	−10.2	−13.8	−12.6	−3.6	−12.2	−13.3
Mali	27.1	36.1	39.4	40.4	40.4	40.4	−5.2	−2.2	−8.2	−6.9	−6.2	−5.5
Mauritius	104.3	156.8	160.0	142.8	130.8	131.0	−5.8	−8.8	−13.3	−13.5	−8.2	−6.8
Mozambique	33.5	43.3	43.6	43.7	43.5	42.2	−31.1	−27.3	−22.8	−36.0	−13.3	−34.6
Namibia	58.3	71.6	71.4	70.4	69.7	69.6	−8.1	2.6	−9.8	−13.5	−5.3	−3.7
Niger	17.5	19.2	20.1	19.7	20.8	20.8	−12.6	−13.2	−14.1	−15.5	−12.8	−8.1
Nigeria	24.3	25.2	25.2	25.8	27.3	28.7	1.2	−3.7	−0.4	−0.7	−0.6	−0.5
Rwanda	22.4	29.4	30.4	30.4	29.9	30.5	−10.5	−12.1	−10.9	−11.6	−13.2	−12.0
São Tomé & Príncipe	36.6	32.5	29.4	27.9	26.3	26.3	−15.6	−11.0	−11.2	−13.8	−11.8	−11.3
Senegal	34.6	45.3	47.8	49.0	49.7	50.0	−7.2	−10.9	−13.6	−16.0	−10.4	−4.6
Seychelles	66.9	113.3	108.2	101.6	101.8	100.9	−15.7	−13.5	−10.4	−7.3	−9.2	−10.0
Sierra Leone	22.2	29.5	32.4	33.9	30.0	28.0	−21.9	−7.1	−8.7	−10.3	−6.1	−5.1
South Africa	66.4	74.1	70.3	71.8	71.9	72.7	−3.5	2.0	3.7	−0.5	−2.3	−2.6
South Sudan	20.7	18.4	14.9	9.6	10.2	10.3	4.5	−19.2	−9.5	6.7	6.3	5.7
Tanzania	22.1	20.9	21.3	21.0	20.9	20.8	−7.0	−1.9	−3.4	−4.6	−4.0	−3.3
Togo	37.6	45.4	47.5	49.1	50.4	51.0	−5.1	−0.3	−0.9	−2.8	−4.0	−3.7
Uganda	17.4	22.4	21.8	20.7	20.6	20.7	−5.7	−9.5	−8.3	−8.1	−10.9	−11.9
Zambia	21.0	31.3	24.3	24.3	24.2	23.9	0.3	10.6	9.2	2.4	3.8	4.5
Zimbabwe[1]	24.1	14.8	14.9	16.0	13.5	13.9	−7.9	2.5	1.0	0.8	0.4	0.8
Sub-Saharan Africa	**35.3**	**38.6**	**37.2**	**36.7**	**36.6**	**36.9**	**−2.7**	**−2.8**	**−1.1**	**−2.0**	**−2.6**	**−2.7**
Median	26.4	31.2	31.1	31.8	30.0	30.5	−5.5	−4.2	−4.2	−4.7	−5.0	−4.6
Excluding Nigeria and South Africa	28.1	32.6	31.4	30.0	29.4	29.4	−4.5	−4.1	−3.3	−3.1	−3.5	−3.7
Oil-exporting countries	**25.3**	**27.2**	**25.2**	**24.9**	**26.1**	**27.1**	**0.9**	**−3.2**	**0.7**	**1.8**	**0.5**	**−0.2**
Excluding Nigeria	27.5	32.0	25.2	22.5	22.8	23.1	0.2	−1.7	3.2	7.0	2.8	0.4
Oil-importing countries	**41.6**	**44.9**	**43.6**	**43.0**	**42.1**	**41.9**	**−5.2**	**−2.6**	**−1.9**	**−4.1**	**−4.2**	**−4.1**
Excluding South Africa	28.2	32.7	32.7	31.6	30.8	30.7	−6.4	−4.6	−4.7	−5.7	−5.0	−4.7
Middle-income countries	**38.4**	**42.1**	**39.9**	**39.7**	**39.7**	**40.2**	**−1.5**	**−1.8**	**0.2**	**−0.6**	**−1.5**	**−1.6**
Excluding Nigeria and South Africa	30.8	36.1	32.9	31.3	30.6	30.6	−2.1	−2.8	−1.9	−0.7	−1.8	−2.0
Low-income countries	**24.6**	**28.7**	**29.6**	**28.5**	**28.2**	**28.2**	**−8.0**	**−5.5**	**−4.9**	**−5.8**	**−5.3**	**−5.5**
Excluding low-income countries in fragile and conflict-affected situations	21.6	24.6	24.8	25.5	25.1	25.3	−8.0	−6.8	−5.9	−6.4	−7.2	−6.9
Countries in fragile and conflict-affected situations	**25.1**	**27.7**	**28.3**	**27.9**	**28.7**	**29.5**	**−1.7**	**−3.8**	**−1.8**	**−2.2**	**−2.0**	**−2.2**
CFA franc zone	22.0	27.7	29.5	28.8	29.1	29.4	−3.7	−3.6	−4.7	−4.4	−4.8	−4.3
CEMAC	20.5	25.9	26.4	26.0	26.8	27.5	−3.3	−2.8	−2.1	2.1	−1.4	−2.9
WAEMU	23.0	28.7	31.1	30.1	30.2	30.2	−4.3	−4.0	−6.2	−8.4	−6.8	−5.1
COMESA (SSA members)	30.1	34.5	33.8	32.2	31.2	31.2	−5.7	−4.1	−3.7	−4.2	−4.6	−4.2
EAC-5	27.4	29.2	28.4	27.4	26.8	26.8	−7.0	−5.1	−5.6	−5.8	−6.4	−6.3
ECOWAS	24.2	27.0	27.4	27.6	28.2	29.0	−1.0	−4.2	−2.4	−3.0	−2.6	−2.0
SACU	64.6	72.4	68.5	69.7	69.9	70.5	−3.4	1.6	3.1	−0.7	−2.1	−2.2
SADC	49.6	54.7	50.8	50.6	50.0	50.1	−3.4	−0.1	1.9	−0.4	−1.6	−2.4

See sources on page 16.

Table SA4. External Debt, Official Debt, Debtor Based and Reserves

	External Debt, Official Debt, Debtor Based (Percent of GDP)						Reserves (Months of imports of goods and services)					
	2011–19	2020	2021	2022	2023	2024	2011–19	2020	2021	2022	2023	2024
Angola	33.6	90.9	68.9	44.2	46.2	45.9	9.3	9.5	7.1	6.8	6.5	6.8
Benin[1]	15.6	30.3	35.2	38.3	38.7	38.1	...	...	...	...	...	...
Botswana	15.4	12.5	10.1	10.4	10.9	9.5	11.4	6.5	6.3	6.6	6.8	7.2
Burkina Faso[1]	20.2	24.4	24.0	25.4	24.7	23.9	...	...	...	...	...	...
Burundi	19.5	17.5	19.9	19.3	27.6	28.8	2.5	1.0	2.3	1.5	2.2	3.4
Cabo Verde	85.5	130.3	114.9	108.1	101.1	98.2	5.7	6.9	6.8	6.2	6.2	6.5
Cameroon[2]	18.4	32.5	30.3	32.9	30.5	29.3	...	...	...	...	...	...
Central African Republic[2]	29.2	36.3	32.8	34.4	31.8	30.7	...	...	...	...	...	...
Chad[2]	24.2	28.2	24.4	23.0	21.8	21.7	...	...	...	...	...	...
Comoros	17.2	23.1	24.5	28.4	31.6	34.8	7.1	7.9	9.4	7.4	7.5	7.7
Congo, Democratic Republic of the	14.1	13.8	14.8	13.4	10.1	8.3	1.0	0.6	0.8	1.1	1.5	1.9
Congo, Republic of [2]	25.4	31.9	26.6	27.0	27.1	24.9	...	...	...	...	...	...
Côte d'Ivoire[1]	19.6	33.6	30.8	36.1	36.7	35.9	...	...	...	...	...	...
Equatorial Guinea[2]	8.8	16.3	12.2	8.4	9.0	9.0	...	...	...	...	...	...
Eritrea	62.2	57.3	55.2	51.2	45.8	42.8	4.7	4.0	4.1	4.5	5.0	5.3
Eswatini	8.8	15.2	15.2	18.6	19.3	19.8	3.7	3.1	3.1	2.4	2.4	2.4
Ethiopia	25.4	28.2	29.1	23.0	18.2	15.8	2.0	2.0	1.5	0.7	0.6	0.5
Gabon[2]	29.8	49.0	36.1	31.1	33.1	32.4	...	...	...	...	...	...
The Gambia	37.5	49.4	47.5	48.3	44.7	42.0	3.6	5.8	7.0	5.1	4.5	4.2
Ghana	26.3	39.2	38.2	42.7	51.8	54.1	2.8	2.5	2.4	0.6	0.8	1.7
Guinea	23.2	27.0	24.8	21.9	19.5	20.4	2.2	1.9	2.5	2.5	2.5	2.5
Guinea-Bissau[1]	30.0	43.9	38.2	40.0	36.7	34.9	...	...	...	...	...	...
Kenya	23.6	32.2	32.3	31.9	33.5	33.9	4.6	4.5	4.7	3.7	3.0	3.3
Lesotho	35.3	46.6	41.0	42.5	44.6	44.5	4.8	4.1	5.1	4.0	4.5	5.6
Liberia	18.4	41.1	37.2	37.2	38.1	38.1	2.1	2.2	4.1	3.5	3.5	3.5
Madagascar	23.4	36.4	37.2	38.9	39.9	39.9	3.4	4.8	4.5	3.8	3.7	3.6
Malawi	19.4	31.8	30.9	29.9	33.2	34.4	2.5	0.9	0.4	1.1	1.3	2.8
Mali[1]	22.8	31.5	27.2	26.7	25.1	23.9	...	...	...	...	...	...
Mauritius	13.3	20.2	23.3	23.5	24.5	23.8	8.4	14.4	12.5	12.1	10.0	9.8
Mozambique	63.8	90.7	85.1	76.1	72.7	73.6	3.5	4.7	2.6	2.9	2.1	2.1
Namibia	12.6	21.3	15.7	17.2	16.9	15.5	3.4	4.1	4.5	4.6	4.7	4.8
Niger[1]	18.4	33.0	31.5	33.0	32.7	30.9	...	...	...	...	...	...
Nigeria	3.7	8.0	9.1	9.4	9.4	9.4	6.1	6.6	6.0	5.7	6.0	6.3
Rwanda	28.0	54.7	53.4	51.5	55.7	61.7	3.9	5.4	4.4	3.7	3.7	4.1
São Tomé & Príncipe	75.1	64.9	58.5	58.1	54.8	54.2	3.8	4.5	4.3	3.8	3.7	3.8
Senegal[1]	32.9	48.9	45.8	47.5	43.5	39.9	...	...	...	...	...	...
Seychelles	35.4	38.8	39.5	31.1	33.7	34.1	3.6	3.7	3.7	3.6	3.5	3.6
Sierra Leone	31.6	48.3	48.3	51.0	56.8	53.0	3.2	4.6	6.1	4.6	3.7	3.3
South Africa	15.0	23.4	18.6	20.7	22.0	22.1	5.8	6.4	5.5	5.2	4.8	4.4
South Sudan	...	...	...	...	...	...	1.7	0.1	0.9	0.4	0.5	0.9
Tanzania	25.9	28.4	28.8	27.4	26.3	25.0	4.8	5.3	4.3	3.9	3.8	4.0
Togo[1]	13.4	28.3	25.4	27.5	26.2	26.3	...	...	...	...	...	...
Uganda	16.9	29.8	27.7	26.8	28.9	29.1	4.6	4.3	4.6	3.4	3.4	3.8
Zambia[3]	26.4	66.6	53.9	...	...	...	2.7	1.3	2.9	3.1	3.3	4.2
Zimbabwe[4]	31.7	26.6	19.8	21.5	23.6	26.3	0.5	0.1	1.3	0.4	0.2	0.2
Sub-Saharan Africa	**16.6**	**26.5**	**24.6**	**24.2**	**24.3**	**23.8**	**5.2**	**5.0**	**4.6**	**4.1**	**4.0**	**4.1**
Median	22.8	32.1	30.8	31.1	32.3	31.0	3.8	4.3	4.3	3.7	3.7	3.8
Excluding Nigeria and South Africa	24.4	36.6	33.9	31.8	31.4	30.4	4.3	3.7	3.6	3.1	2.9	3.1
Oil-exporting countries	**11.2**	**20.1**	**19.5**	**18.0**	**17.9**	**17.8**	**6.3**	**6.4**	**5.6**	**5.5**	**5.8**	**6.1**
Excluding Nigeria	27.6	55.8	45.4	36.1	36.8	36.5	6.7	5.6	4.8	5.1	5.2	5.5
Oil-importing countries	**20.3**	**29.9**	**27.2**	**27.6**	**27.7**	**27.1**	**4.4**	**4.3**	**4.0**	**3.4**	**3.1**	**3.1**
Excluding South Africa	23.7	32.9	31.4	30.7	30.1	29.0	3.5	3.3	3.3	2.5	2.4	2.6
Middle-income countries	**14.7**	**25.2**	**23.2**	**23.2**	**23.9**	**23.7**	**5.8**	**5.8**	**5.2**	**4.9**	**4.8**	**5.0**
Excluding Nigeria and South Africa	24.6	42.0	37.9	35.7	37.1	36.5	5.4	4.6	4.3	4.0	3.8	4.2
Low-income countries	**24.5**	**30.5**	**29.1**	**27.1**	**25.2**	**24.1**	**2.8**	**2.8**	**2.7**	**2.0**	**1.9**	**2.0**
Excluding low-income countries in fragile and conflict-affected situations	22.5	32.0	31.1	30.1	30.2	30.0	3.9	4.2	3.9	3.4	3.3	3.6
Countries in fragile and conflict-affected situations	**11.1**	**17.2**	**17.4**	**16.7**	**15.7**	**15.3**	**4.8**	**4.8**	**4.4**	**4.0**	**4.0**	**4.2**
CFA franc zone	21.0	33.7	30.8	32.2	31.8	30.9	4.6	4.6	4.4	4.1	3.9	3.9
CEMAC	20.9	33.0	28.2	27.1	26.8	26.2	4.2	3.2	3.0	4.2	4.3	4.5
WAEMU	21.3	34.1	32.3	35.3	34.6	33.4	4.9	5.4	5.2	4.1	3.6	3.7
COMESA (SSA members)	22.2	30.2	29.1	26.7	25.4	24.0	3.2	3.1	3.1	2.5	2.2	2.4
EAC-5	23.1	31.5	31.3	30.4	31.4	31.3	4.6	4.7	4.5	3.7	3.4	3.7
ECOWAS	9.9	18.6	19.2	19.7	20.1	20.0	5.1	5.2	4.9	4.3	4.4	4.8
SACU	14.9	23.0	18.3	20.3	21.4	21.4	5.9	6.3	5.4	5.3	4.9	4.6
SADC	20.4	32.2	27.0	26.4	26.9	26.5	5.7	5.6	4.8	4.7	4.4	4.4

See sources on page 16.